Why *Voting* Matters

What Is Voting?

Kristen Rajczak Nelson

NEW YORK

Published in 2019 by The Rosen Publishing Group, Inc.
29 East 21st Street, New York, NY 10010

Editor: Elizabeth Krajnik
Book Design: Rachel Rising

Photo Credits: Cover Hero Images/Hero Images/Getty Images; Cover (background), pp. 1, 3, 4, 6, 8, 10, 12, 14, 16, 18, 20, 22, 23, 24 (background) PepinoVerde/Shutterstock.com; p. 5 Africa Studio/Shutterstock.com; p. 7 Monkey Business Images/Shutterstock.com; p. 9 plherrera/iStockphoto.com; pp. 11, 21 The Washington Post/The Washington Post/Getty Images; p. 13 Joseph Sohm/Shutterstock.com; p. 15 Rob Crandall/Shutterstock.com; p. 17 PUNIT PARANJPE/AFP/Getty Images; p. 19 Hill Street Studios/Blend Images/Getty Images; p. 22 Daniel Hurst Photography/Photographer's Choice/Getty Images.

Cataloging-in-Publication Data

Names: Rajczak Nelson, Kristen.
Title: What is voting? / Kristen Rajczak Nelson.
Description: New York : PowerKids Press, 2019. | Series: Why voting matters | Includes index.
Identifiers: LCCN ISBN 9781538330135 (pbk.) | ISBN 9781538330111 (library bound) | ISBN 9781538330142 (6 pack)
Subjects: LCSH: Voting--United States--Juvenile literature. | Elections--United States--Juvenile literature. | Political participation--United States--Juvenile literature.
Classification: LCC JK1978.R35 2019 | DDC 324.60973--dc23

Manufactured in the United States of America

CPSIA Compliance Information: Batch #CS18PK For further information contact Rosen Publishing, New York, New York at 1-800-237-9932.

Contents

The Right to Vote

One of the **benefits** of being a **citizen** of the United States is the promise of exercising certain rights. The U.S. **Constitution** and its **amendments** state these rights. One of the most important is the right to vote. Many Americans view this as a **civic** duty and take great pride in it.

Make a Choice

When members of a group of people each make a choice and each person's choice is counted, that's voting. You may have voted by simply raising your hand in class to pick what movie to watch. Some TV shows let fans call in, text, or visit a website to vote for winners each week.

It's Official

When people talk about voting, they most often mean making an **official** choice for a government leader. When many people vote at the same time, it's called an election. Voters visit polling places during elections. Polling places are buildings, such as churches and fire stations, where people gather to vote.

Kinds of Ballots

At a polling place, voters use a **ballot** to make their choice. Ballots can be made of paper. Paper ballots are counted by hand or read by a machine. In some states, voters use computers to cast their vote. Voters press a button or touch the screen to make their choice.

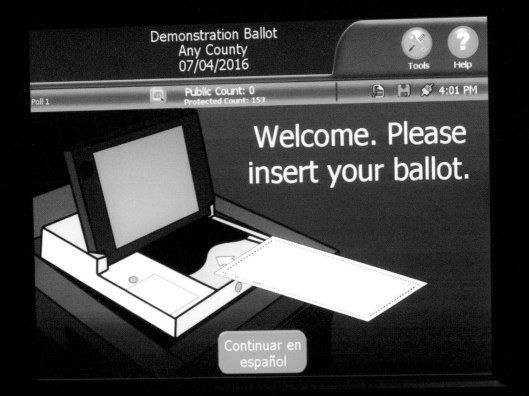

11

Becoming a Voter

U.S. voters must be citizens who turn 18 years old on or before the next Election Day. They also must be **registered** to vote. In order to register in a state, a person needs to live in that state for a certain amount of time. The amount of time is different from state to state.

13

When to Vote

Most people vote on the day of an election. Many states allow people to vote before that, too. Early voting helps more people vote in an election. They might even be able to vote weeks ahead of the election. The rules about early voting are different from state to state.

15

Absentee Voting

Every state gives out ballots to people who can't vote the day of the election. This may be because they live outside their home state. These are called absentee ballots. U.S. citizens living in other countries and people in the military often vote by absentee ballot. It's still voting even though the voters aren't there in person!

Primary Elections

Before a major election, such as a presidential election, some states have special kinds of elections called primaries. In a primary election, voters choose one person from each **political party** to run in the larger election. In some states, people can only vote in primary elections if they belong to a political party. People commonly vote in a primary in the same way they do in other elections.

19

Count for the Win

After voters send in their absentee ballots or go to a polling place, votes are counted. Most often, the person who receives the most votes is the winner. In this way, voters choose many people who serve in government, such as mayors, members of Congress, and local **representatives**.

Voters' Voices

Voters never have to pay to vote. All voting is done in secret. Though most citizens over age 18 have the right to vote, some people choose not to vote. No one is forced to vote. Voting is important because it gives citizens a say in who will speak for them in government!

Glossary

amendment: A change in the words or meaning of a law or official paper, such as a constitution.

ballot: A vote cast in an election, and sometimes the pieces of paper the votes are cast on.

benefit: Something that produces good or helpful results or effects.

citizen: A person who lives in a country and has the rights given to them by that country's laws.

civic: Of or relating to a city or town or the people who live there.

constitution: The basic laws by which a country, state, or group is governed.

official: Recognized by the government or someone in power.

political party: A group of people with the same ideas about how the government should be run.

register: To put your name on an official list.

representative: A member of a lawmaking body who acts for voters.

Index

Websites

Due to the changing nature of Internet links, PowerKids Press has developed an online list of websites related to the subject of this book. This site is updated regularly. Please use this link to access the list: www.powerkidslinks.com/wvm/wiv